THAILAND

By Sloane Gould and
Joanne Mattern

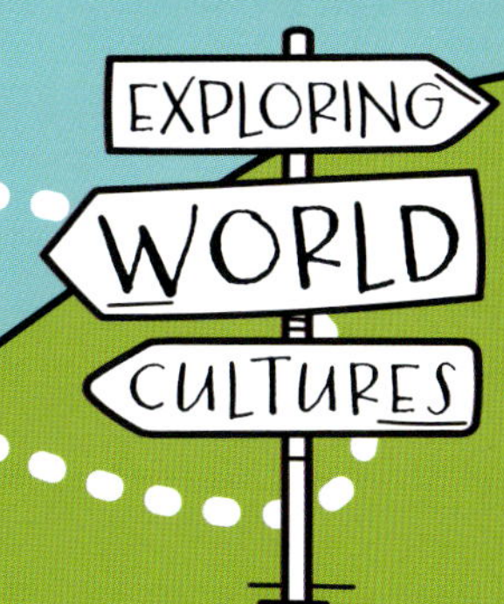

Published in 2026 by Cavendish Square Publishing, LLC
2544 Clinton Street, Buffalo, NY 14224

Second Edition

Website: cavendishsq.com

Library of Congress Cataloging-in-Publication Data

Names: Mattern, Joanne, 1963- author. | Gould, Sloane, author.
Title: Thailand / Joanne Mattern.
Description: Second edition / Sloane Gould. | Buffalo, NY : Cavendish Square Publishing, 2026. | Series: Exploring world cultures | Includes index.
Identifiers: LCCN 2024045356 (print) | LCCN 2024045357 (ebook) | ISBN 9781502673510 (library binding) | ISBN 9781502673503 (paperback) | ISBN 9781502673527 (ebook)
Subjects: LCSH: Thailand--Juvenile literature.
Classification: LCC DS563.5 .M28 2025 (print) | LCC DS563.5 (ebook) | DDC 959.3--dc23/eng/20241114
LC record available at https://lccn.loc.gov/2024045356
LC ebook record available at https://lccn.loc.gov/2024045357

Writers: Joanne Mattern; Sloane Gould (second edition)
Editor: Caitie McAneney
Copyeditor: Jill Keppeler
Designer: Deanna Lepovich

The photographs in this book are used by permission and through the courtesy of: Cover Supermop/Shutterstock.com; p. 4 Kadagan/Shutterstock.com; p. 5 Foto-Kern/Shutterstock.com; p. 6 Nathapon Triratanachat/Shutterstock.com; p. 7 Day2505/Shutterstock.com; p. 8 fokke baarssen/Shutterstock.com; p. 9 amnat30/Shutterstock.com; p. 10 Tatohra/Shutterstock.com; p. 11 sunyaluk/Shutterstock.com; p. 12 ozerkizildag/Shutterstock.com; p. 13 sasirin pamai/Shutterstock.com; p. 15 (top) Baptiste Mauerhan/Shutterstock.com; p. 15 (bottom) MartinJGruber/Shutterstock.com; p. 16 Brostock/Shutterstock.com; p. 17 KobchaiMa/Shutterstock.com; p. 18 itman__47/Shutterstock.com; p. 19 ChungPhotoMan/Shutterstock.com; p. 20 Amonsak/Shutterstock.com; p. 21 drpnncpptak/Shutterstock.com; p. 22 John And Penny/Shutterstock.com; p. 23 Panya_Anakotmankong/Shutterstock.com; p. 24 Gerardo C.Lerner/Shutterstock.com; p. 25 Take Photo/Shutterstock.com; p. 26 JU.STOCKER/Shutterstock.com; p. 27 LANLOM/Shutterstock.com; p. 28 dodotone/Shutterstock.com; p. 29 jaboo2foto/Shutterstock.com.

CPSIA compliance information: Batch #CS26CSQ: For further information contact Cavendish Square Publishing LLC at 1-877-980-4450.

Printed in the United States of America

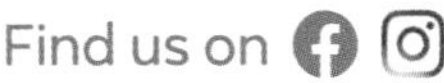

CONTENTS

INTRODUCTION

Thailand is known as the "Land of Smiles." People who live here are called Thai. Thai people are known for being friendly and helpful. That is just one reason why people love to visit Thailand!

Thailand's capital is Bangkok.

Thailand's animal diversity can be seen in Kaeng Krachan National Park. This is a dusky leaf monkey.

Thailand is also home to some of the most beautiful beaches in the world. Southern Thailand is a thin **peninsula** with many beaches. This Southeast Asian country is known for its floating markets and fun celebrations. It's also known for its **diversity** of wildlife, including elephants, leopards, and many more animals.

Thailand has an interesting history. Until the 1930s, it was known as Siam. The name "Thailand" means "land of the free." It's the only Southeast Asian nation that has never been ruled by Europeans. Rich in natural beauty, this country also has a long history of farming. Today, many factories have been built here as more businesses take root in the country. Let's explore the beautiful country of Thailand!

GEOGRAPHY

Thailand is in mainland Southeast Asia. The Thai say that the country is shaped like the head of an elephant. The northern part, which looks like the elephant's head and ear, borders Myanmar, Laos, and Cambodia. The southern part, which looks like the elephant's trunk, is on the Malay Peninsula. Malaysia is to the south, while the Andaman Sea and Gulf of Thailand are on either side.

FACT!

Phuket is the largest island in Thailand. It's in the Andaman Sea.

Thailand is tropical, or warm and wet. Heavy rains happen between May and October.

Northern Thailand is home to huge mountains. Doi Inthanon is Thailand's tallest mountain. It is located near the city of Chiang Mai. It is 8,415 feet (2,565 m) high. Rivers run from the mountains south through the country. The Mekong River flows along Thailand's eastern border. It's very important to people living in Thailand.

THE MEKONG RIVER

The Mekong River separates Thailand from Laos. Many people live and work along the river. They catch fish and grow crops on farms near the water.

These cool rocks are in Phang Nga Bay, near the Thai island of Phuket.

HISTORY

Around 4,000 years ago, people began building communities in Thailand. Many different groups moved there from China and other parts of Asia. A group called the Thai came around 1,000 years ago. The first Thai kingdom was called Sukhothai. It lasted from 1238 to 1438. The area became part of the kingdom of Ayutthaya in the 1300s. It then became known as Siam.

FACT!

*Thailand was hit by a huge **tsunami** in 2004. It took a long time to recover.*

*Wat Arun is Thailand's best-known landmark. This Buddhist **temple** was started in the 1600s.*

In 1511, the first Europeans came to Thailand. At first, the Thai rulers didn't want the Europeans there. In 1851, a ruler named Rama IV welcomed Europeans. Rama IV worked to make Thailand a modern nation. Until 1932, Thailand's kings ruled the country. Then, the nation became a constitutional monarchy with its current name. In a constitutional monarchy, there is a ruler, but they do not have all the power. There is a set of laws called a constitution.

THE FIRST SETTLEMENT

The first Thai settlement is believed to be Ban Chiang in northeast Thailand. People have found signs of early farming and use of metal tools here.

People can discover early Thai **artifacts** at the Ban Chiang National Museum.

GOVERNMENT

Thailand's first constitution went into effect in 1932. However, there have been over a dozen constitutions and changes since then. The Thai constitution divides the government's power between three parts: executive, legislative, and judicial.

THE NATIONAL ASSEMBLY

Thailand's National Assembly is made of two parts, the Senate and House of Representatives. They meet in the Sappaya-Sapasathan building in Bangkok.

The Thai flag has stripes in red, white, and blue.

The executive part includes the king or queen and their advisers. The advisers are called the privy council. The king or queen signs laws and guides ceremonies. It is against the law to say anything bad about the king or queen. The prime minister is also under the executive part. They lead the government. Thailand is divided into 76 parts called provinces. Each province is run by a governor.

FACT!
The highest court in Thailand is the Supreme Court.

The legislative part is known as the National Assembly. This part creates laws. Finally, the judicial part includes Thailand's courts. Courts decide if laws are fair or not.

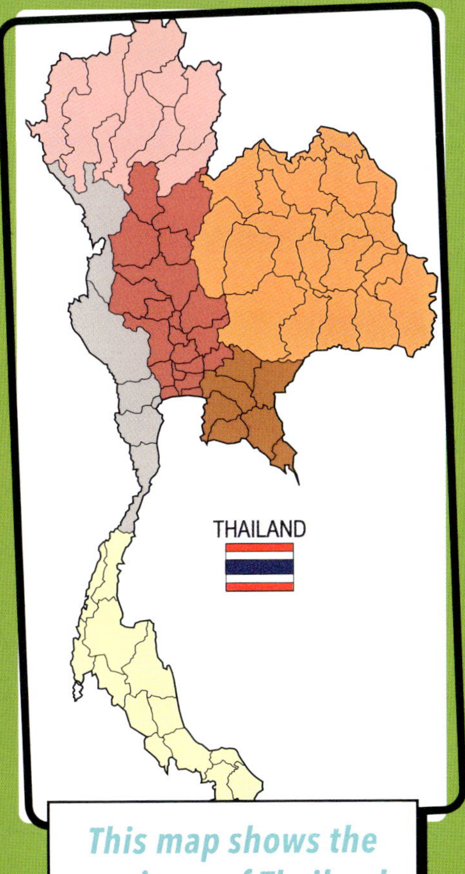

This map shows the provinces of Thailand.

THE ECONOMY

Farming has been an important **industry** in Thailand since its beginnings. While farming is less important today, it still provides jobs and brings in money. Rice is the most important crop. Thailand also grows sugarcane, coconuts, pineapples, and melons. Some farmers sell their crops on boats in floating markets. Some people work in gemstone mines. Rubies and sapphires are mined on Thailand's eastern coast.

Floating markets have been part of Thailand's economy for hundreds of years.

Today, manufacturing and service jobs are the most common. Thailand makes many products, including electronics, cars and trucks, and clothing. Thailand sells most of these goods to other countries.

Service jobs include teachers, bankers, doctors, and government workers. Many Thai people work in hotels, restaurants, stores, and other businesses that help visitors. **Tourism** is one of the most important industries!

FACT!

Thailand is the world's second-largest producer of a metal called tungsten.

Thailand's colorful money is called baht.

TOURISM

In 2023, more than 28 million people visited Thailand! They like to visit beaches, parks, and temples.

THE ENVIRONMENT

Thailand has many plants and animals. It's a tropical nation with beautiful flowers like orchids and lotuses. Northern Thailand has low mountains and thick forests of teak and bamboo trees. The rainforests of Southern Thailand are home to elephants, tigers, and crocodiles. Fruit bats, pythons, king cobras, and monitor lizards also live there. These animals eat birds, rodents, and insects.

Air pollution is a problem in Thailand. It has some of the worst air quality in Southeast Asia. Air pollution comes from cars and factories. The government is working to improve public transportation, such as buses and trains. This may help keep air pollution down in busy places such as Bangkok. Water is also not always clean in Thailand, which is bad for both animals and people.

FACT!

Too much water (flooding) and too little water (drought) are big issues in Thailand.

Flooding may happen more often in Thailand because of ***climate change.***

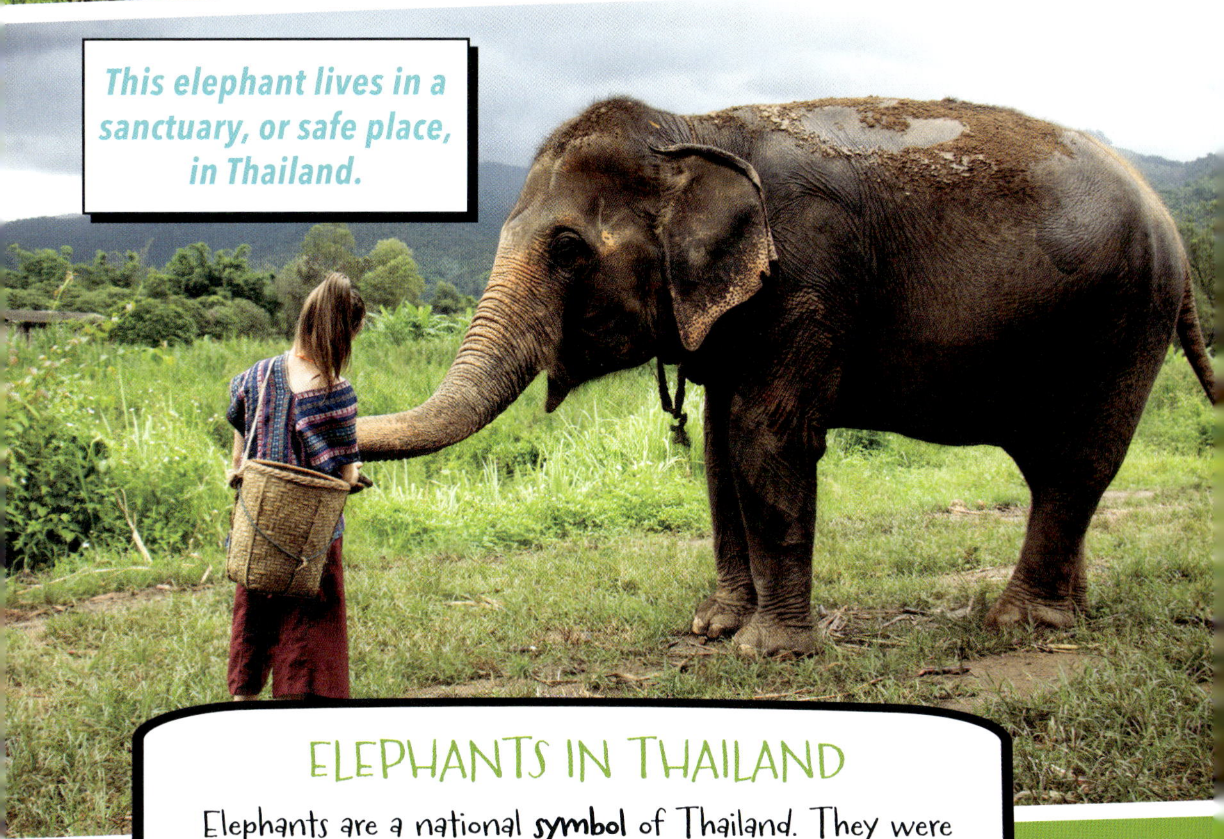

This elephant lives in a sanctuary, or safe place, in Thailand.

ELEPHANTS IN THAILAND

Elephants are a national **symbol** of Thailand. They were once used in battle. Today, they are still used as working animals. Some are protected in safe places called sanctuaries.

THE PEOPLE TODAY

Millions of tourists visit Thailand each year, but nearly 70 million people call Thailand home. Most of them are native Thai. Others can trace their roots back to China, Malaysia, and Myanmar (once known as Burma).

Thai families often enjoy sharing meals together.

MIXED ROOTS

Many people in Thailand have mixed ancestry, or roots. The most common mix is Thai and Chinese. In fact, Rama I, the founder of the current Thai **dynasty**, was part Chinese.

Many people in southern Thailand are Malay. The Malay people have lived on land that is now part of Thailand for hundreds of years. They speak a different language and have different **traditions** than most Thai people. Beginning in 1939, the Thai government has forced Malay Muslims (followers of Islam) to speak the Thai language and follow certain rules. This has led to **conflict**, especially in the past 20 years.

Several different groups live in Thailand's northern and western provinces. They are called hill tribes. Their ancestors came to Thailand from Laos, Myanmar, Tibet, and China.

FACT!

Most Malay people in Thailand practice the religion called Islam.

This village is home to a hill tribe.

LIFESTYLE

Life in Thailand is different in the country and the city. More than 11 million people live in the city of Bangkok. These people usually live in small apartments. Bangkok's streets are very crowded. People ride on buses, *tuk-tuks*, or motorcycles. Trains connect cities to towns in the countryside.

FACT!

People who live in hill villages have very different lifestyles than other Thai people.

This three-wheeled vehicle is called a tuk-tuk.

SCHOOL IN THAILAND

Thai children must go to school from ages 7 to 16. Many then complete three more years of upper secondary school to get into a university. Others go to school to learn a trade.

About half of all Thai people live in the countryside. Many families here live in raised houses. They are built on poles, or stilts, so they do not flood during the rainy season. People may be farmers, growing crops like rice, or fishermen.

The traditional Thai dress is called **chut thai.**

Thai parents usually have around one or two children. These children usually live with their parents until they are married. In the past 10 years, more Thai women have gone to college than men. However, only about 59 percent of Thai women are in the workforce, compared to about 75 percent of men.

RELIGION

Buddhism has a long history in Thailand. Today, more than 92 percent of Thai people are Buddhist. They follow the teachings of the Buddha, who was also known as Siddhartha Gautama. He lived around 2,400 years ago in India. He believed that every living thing goes through a cycle of birth, death, and rebirth. By doing good deeds, a person can break this cycle and achieve true freedom.

FACT!

Followers of the religion, or faith, of Islam gather at mosques.

Wat Mahathat is from the Ayutthaya Kingdom in the 14th century.

Just about every Thai village has a Buddhist temple, called a wat. Wats are in cities too. Famous wats include Wat Mahathat and Wat Arun. Many families have statues, or models, of Buddha at home. They place gifts like food in front of Buddha for good luck and health. Many Thai men become Buddhist monks, or men who spend their days studying Buddhism and doing good works.

Wat Traimit in Bangkok holds a famous solid-gold Buddha.

BUDDHIST MONKS

Buddhist monks wear orange robes. They live a simple life that is very different from life in a big city in Thailand or anywhere else.

LANGUAGE

Most people in Thailand speak the official language—Thai. It is a difficult language to learn. One word can have different meanings. The meaning of a word changes depending on the tone of the speaker's voice. The Thai alphabet was created by a king in the late 1200s. Thai has 44 consonants and 32 vowels. There are no spaces between words when Thai is written down.

FACT!

Thai has five different tones to show the meaning of a word.

This sign has both Thai and English letters on it.

A small part of the population also speaks Burmese. This language comes from Thailand's neighbor, Myanmar. Others speak Malay, which comes from Malaysia. English is also spoken in Thailand. It is mostly used by businesspeople for work. Because there are so many tourists in Thailand, signs are often written in both English and Thai.

TAI LUE LANGUAGE

A small number of people living in northern Thailand speak a language called Tai Lu. This language comes from the Tai Lue **ethnic** group spread across China, Laos, Myanmar, and Thailand.

Learning a language is not easy!

ARTS AND FESTIVALS

Traditional arts in Thailand often have to do with Buddhism. Buddha is often shown in statues, paintings, pottery, and woven silk. Thai people have long been known for the beautiful products they make from silk, gems, and silver. Today, art and music are often a mix of Thai and western styles. People visit the Museum of Contemporary Art (MOCA) to check out exciting new Thai artwork.

FACT!

The Thai New Year is celebrated with a festival called Songkran. Some people take part in fun water fights during Songkran!

Traditional Thai art can be seen in wats around the country.

The Thai people celebrate many Buddhist holidays. Vassa takes place from July to October. During this time, many Buddhists give up things like eating meat. Visakha Puja, also known as Vesak, is the most important Buddhist holiday. It is celebrated in May and honors Buddha's life. People get together in wats to sing and listen to speeches. At night, they may walk around a temple's hall three times while carrying flowers and candles.

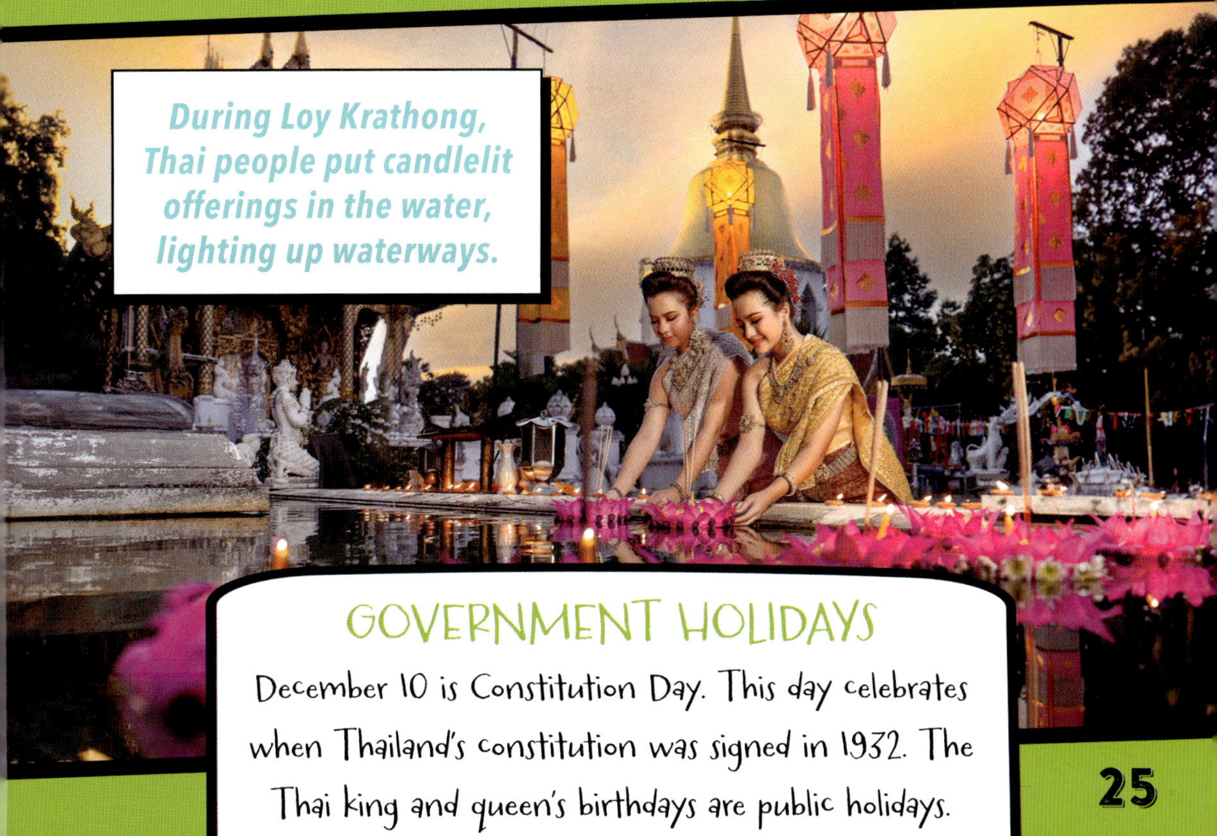

During Loy Krathong, Thai people put candlelit offerings in the water, lighting up waterways.

GOVERNMENT HOLIDAYS

December 10 is Constitution Day. This day celebrates when Thailand's constitution was signed in 1932. The Thai king and queen's birthdays are public holidays.

FUN AND PLAY

Martial arts are important in Thailand. Muay Thai is the national sport. It is a martial art that is a lot like kickboxing. It was created out of fighting tactics, or actions, from the Thai army. In the early 1900s, people started using boxing gloves in this sport.

FACT!

Muay Thai has been a sport since around 1700.

This fighter is ready to practice Muay Thai.

One of Thailand's best Olympic sports is boxing. Boxer Somluck Kamsing was the first Thai Olympian to win a gold medal. He won at the 1996 Summer Olympics in Atlanta, Georgia. Other popular sports are soccer, table tennis, basketball, and gymnastics.

Many Thai people enjoy flying kites, especially during windy days in the spring. A kite can be any shape, size, or color. Sometimes people have battles and try to knock other kites out of the sky. In fact, kite flying is a sport in Thailand!

People have flown kites for sport in Thailand for hundreds of years.

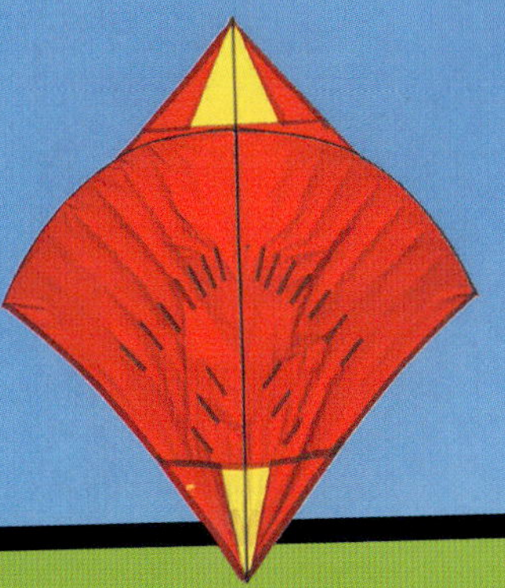

TAKRAW

Takraw is another popular sport. It is a lot like volleyball, but players cannot use their hands or arms. Many children enjoy playing takraw.

FOOD

Thai food is known around the world for its bold flavors. Many dishes use all five tastes: sweet, sour, salty, savory, and bitter. Spicy chilies are a common ingredient, along with many herbs and spices. Curry is a favorite food in Thailand. It is a stew that often mixes meat, green chilies, vegetables, and coconut rice. Satay, or grilled meat on a stick, is a popular snack in Thailand.

FACT!

Many people consider Thailand's national dish to be pad thai, which includes fried rice noodles.

Many people buy food at street markets in Thailand.

Rice is part of almost every meal. Thai rice is sticky. It is often flavored with coconut milk and eaten with fish, meat, or vegetables. Rice noodles that are wide and flat are also included in some dishes.

For dessert, people in Thailand may eat a sweet dish called mango sticky rice. Coconut lovers use this tropical fruit in custards and pancakes.

***Luk chup** is a Thai dessert made from mung beans to look like tiny, colorful fruits.*

THAI TEA

Tea is a popular drink in Thailand. Some people enjoy it with sweetened milk. Others like their tea mixed with lime juice.

GLOSSARY

artifact: Something made by humans in the past that still exists.

climate change: Change in Earth's weather over a long period of time caused by human activity.

conflict: A fight, battle, or war.

diversity: The quality or state of having many different types, forms, or ideas.

dynasty: A line of rulers who belong to the same family.

ethnic: Relating to large groups of people who have the same origin, religion, customs, and more.

industry: The businesses in an area.

peninsula: A landform that is surrounded by water on three sides.

symbol: Something that stands for something else.

temple: A building that is sacred, or holy, to a religious group.

tourism: The business of drawing in tourists, or people traveling to visit another place.

tradition: A way of thinking, behaving, or doing something that's been used by people in a particular society for a long time.

tsunami: A huge sea wave caused by an earthquake.

FIND OUT MORE

Books

Davies, Monika. *Thailand*. Minneapolis, MN: Bellwether Media, Inc., 2024.

Mather, Charis. *A Visit to Thailand*. Minneapolis, MN: Bearport Publishing, 2023.

Orr, Tamara. *Thailand*. New York, NY: Lightbox Learning, 2025.

Websites

Thailand
kids.britannica.com/kids/article/Thailand/345800
Explore more interesting facts about Thailand with Britannica Kids.

Thailand Facts
www.kids-world-travel-guide.com/thailand-facts.html
Learn facts about Thailand, written for kids by kids!

Video

Asia | Destination World
www.youtube.com/watch?v=nsOtOye-DJM
Learn more about the continent of Asia—home to Thailand.

INDEX